The Christian and Habitual Sin

How to Gain Deliverance by God's Grace

Thomas W. Bear

*"We know that our old self was crucified with him so that the body of sin might be done away with, **that we should no longer be slaves to sin**" (Romans 6:6).*

Copyright notices

The Christian and Habitual Sin: How to Gain Deliverance by God's Grace

Acknowledgments

For their contributions and support in writing this book, I want to thank my wife Linda, Jim "The Captain," Marilyn Delpaz, Rubin Orr, Mike Mathis, Michelle Peters, Jason Jones and Patrick McMahon.

Contents

Introduction

Before proceeding, it must be noted that many people falsely assume they are Christians while according to the Bible, they are not actually Christians at all. If as you read through this booklet, you find its teachings to be strange, consider the possibility that you might not actually be a Christian. If there is any question in your mind about this, let me suggest that you review the material in the Appendix, "The gospel of Jesus Christ." If you do not believe the gospel of Jesus Christ <u>from the heart</u>, you are not a Christian and must not expect to find sustained deliverance from habitual sin. Many people believe the gospel with their mind and assume that they are Christians. They can recite the "Apostles Creed" and affirm it as true. It is not sufficient to merely agree with the gospel. If you do not believe the gospel of Jesus Christ <u>from the heart</u>, you have a bigger problem. You are separated from God and under condemnation. Your greatest need is that you believe the gospel from the heart so that you can be reconciled to God and receive eternal life.

All true Christians have been born again, made alive by God's grace. They believe the gospel of Jesus Christ from the heart. The Holy Spirit lives inside them and is at work to produce holy lives full of love, peace, patience, and many other characteristics that reflect the very nature of God. The instruction provided by this booklet is mainly addressed to <u>Christians</u> (those who have the life of Jesus in them) and based upon truth directly from the Bible. The truth within it can indeed produce deliverance but only to those who have the life of Jesus in them.

Jesus came not only to deliver us from the **penalty of sin** (eternal damnation), He also came to deliver us from the **bondage of sin** (slavery to it). Jesus said that He came to give abundant life. (See John 10:10.[1]) In light of this, what if a Christian finds himself habitually committing acts that the Bible classifies as sinful? Perhaps he is in the habit of viewing pornography and gratifying his own sexual lusts. Perhaps he has a drug or alcohol habit. Every Christian falls into some type of sin during his lifetime. Normally, the Christian sees the error of his way and repents. But what happens if, instead, he finds himself stuck, committing that sin day in and day out as a habit that seems impossible to break?

The Apostle Paul taught that Christians are no longer slaves of sin. (See Romans 6:6.[2]) Slavery to habitual sin is a contradiction to the Christian life described by the Bible. So, when habitual sins plague a Christian, peace is replaced with turmoil and confusion. **If** you are a Christian caught in habitual sin, you undoubtedly long for deliverance from it. This little booklet was written to help Christians gain deliverance from habitual sins.

---

[1] "The thief cometh not, but for to steal, and to kill, and to destroy: <u>I am come that they might have life, and that they might have it more abundantly</u>" (John 10:10 KJV).

[2] "Knowing this, that our old self was crucified with Him, in order that our body of sin might be done away with, <u>so that we would no longer be slaves to sin</u>" (Romans 6:6 NASB).

Deliverance comes at a cost.

Try to envision your life in the future, free from the sin that now encumbers you. What does that life look like in your mind? Does it look pretty much the same as it does now except free of the sin that plagues you? Let me suggest that if this is how you imagine it, the picture is distorted. If you are serious about gaining deliverance, you need to realize that radical changes must take place in your thinking and behavior and that these changes are not possible apart from the miraculous work of God.

The Bible speaks of a principle that is a key to deliverance from sin. For every sin we "put off," we must put on a virtuous behavior that acts as a replacement. In the fourth chapter of Paul's epistle to the Ephesians, he says to put off lying and begin speaking truth. He says to put off stealing and begin laboring so that we might be able to give to others who are in need. He says to stop using corrupt language, and begin speaking only those things that edify. We are to put off the old way of living and put on the new man which is created in righteousness and holiness. (See Ephesians 4:17-32.)

You should not expect sustained deliverance from a sin that has occupied much of your existence without it being replaced with a virtuous behavior that becomes food for your soul. Your soul longs for food. You can either feed it garbage that destroys it or food that God has provided to nourish it. Your soul's taste buds must be re-trained to enjoy those things that produce the true life of Jesus. Your flesh loves the garbage you have been feeding it so training your soul's taste buds will require God's grace to be unleashed in your life.

The radical changes that must take place in your behavior must begin with radical changes in your thinking. What I am about to say applies to every Christian, but especially to anyone who seeks deliverance from a habitual sin. If you think that deliverance is possible through a series of steps, you will likely be frustrated by repeated failure.

If you sincerely want deliverance from a habitual sin, please consider this heart-felt word of admonition. Briefly, I wish to communicate the following things:

1. In general, the type of Christianity on display in North America is highly dysfunctional and anemic. This is true even in churches that most Christians would consider to be strong, healthy and vibrant.

2. Unless you are way outside the norm, you need a complete change in your thinking about what it means to be a Christian. You cannot settle for the type of life that is being lived by most Christians in North America. This will not do for you.

3. If you want deliverance from habitual sin, you must discard your old way of living the Christian life and begin to live it as the Bible describes it, not as it is being modeled in North America.

4. **Chiefly**, you must become an aggressive, active participant in the advancement of God's Kingdom. You must set your mind to seek God's direction in this matter as it concerns you personally. Once you ascertain God's purposes for you personally, you must begin fulfilling His purposes as if your eternal destiny depends on it. In other words, finishing your God-given mission should be viewed as mandatory in your pursuit of heaven. Deserting your God-assigned mission and settling once again for dysfunctional Christian living should be viewed as the path to hell. (Try not to assume things about my theology on the basis for what I just said. Hopefully, you will better understand why I say it this way as you continue reading the book.) If what I have said so far seems over the top to you, then perhaps you are not quite ready to lay hold of the deliverance that Jesus purchased for you when He died on the cross. More will be said about this later in the section, ***Do God's will as one who is advancing His Kingdom.***

In order to provide the help that is foundational for deliverance, we will first examine the eternal danger of habitual sin in general. (Unless you first comprehend the seriousness of habitual sin, you may not be properly motivated to seek God for deliverance from it.) After this, we will address the steps described in the Bible that, if followed, can guide you to sustained deliverance.

A lifestyle of habitual sin will have eternal consequences.

The Bible states that all people who live lives that are enslaved to sin will not inherit the kingdom of God. *"Now the **deeds of the flesh** are evident, which are: immorality, impurity, sensuality, idolatry, sorcery, **enmities, strife, jealousy, outbursts of anger, disputes, dissensions, factions, envying, drunkenness, carousing,** and things like these, of which I forewarn you, just as I have forewarned you, that those who practice such things **will not inherit the kingdom of God"** (Galatians 5:19-21 NASB).* It doesn't matter how often a person attends church. If he is, and **continues to be**, enslaved to sin (one who "practices" one of these sins), he will not inherit eternal life. (See also I Corinthians 6:9-10 & Revelation 21:8). Alcohol abuse, drug abuse and sexual sins are not the only sins that have serious consequences. Overeating and a bad temper may also fall into the category of dangerous habitual sins from which we need deliverance.

Many people who profess to know Christ struggle with habitual sin. Perhaps you are one of them. Since the Bible explicitly warns that those who are enslaved to sin will perish, let us consider the danger of habitual sin and then God's remedy for it.

What types of sin, if "practiced," have eternal consequences?

According to the Apostle Paul, if your life is dominated by "works of the flesh," you have great reason to be concerned where you will spend eternity. Most professing Christians look at passages like Galatians 5:19 - 21 and focus on the more overt sinful behavior such as murder, adultery or homosexuality. They don't consider that less blatant forms of dominant sinful behavior and attitudes such as selfish ambitions, hot tempers, addiction to pornography and self-gratification can also send people to hell.

Brief definitions of the sins listed in Galatians 5:19 - 21 are provided below:

Immorality: *sexual relations/activity that is condemned by God (sex outside of marriage)*

Impurity: *uncleanness, letting one's heart and mind engage in sexual lust and imaginations*

Sensuality: *licentiousness, wantonness, to let the desire for sensual pleasure occupy the heart without restraint*

Idolatry: *desiring things other than God more than God himself (including money)*

Sorcery: *the use of drugs, spells, to engage in spiritual activities that are associated with the kingdom of darkness*

Enmities: *hostile mindset towards another person or other people in general*

Strife: *to quarrel with other people*

Jealousy: *zeal to possess the sole affection of someone that you think is yours already*

Outbursts of anger: *angry tempers, indignation, rage, wrath*

Disputes: *rivalry, selfish ambition, selfishness*

Dissensions: *standing apart, stubborn*

Factions: *stubbornly holding to one's opinion without biblical support for doing so; heresies*

Envying: *zeal to possess something or someone that belongs to another already*

Drunkenness: *being intoxicated to the point that one is controlled by the substance*

Carousing: *to revel, to 'party,' looking to enjoy the world's pleasures with a lustful heart*

How can we tell if we are one of those who "practice" these things?

If a man commits adultery, is he destined for hell? If a person has an outburst of anger or selfish ambitions, does that mean he "practices" these sins? From the account of King David's sin with Bathsheba, we know that David committed flagrant adultery and even murdered the husband of Bathsheba to cover up his sin. (See II Samuel 11:1-12:14.[3]) Yet, David, the writer of many of the Psalms, knew God and was called a man after God's own heart. (See I Samuel 13:14.[4]) We conclude that a single act of adultery and even murder does not necessarily disqualify a person for the Kingdom of God. Crossing a certain line of gross sinful behavior does not necessarily disqualify us for heaven. We see from King David's life that it is possible for a believer to experience a period in their life in which they are "caught in sin."

Galatians 6:1 says, *"If someone is **caught in a sin**, you who are spiritual should restore him gently."* James indicates that it is possible for a Christian to *"wander from the truth" (James 5:19).*

---

[3] *"It came to pass, after the year was expired, at the time when kings go forth to battle, that David sent Joab, and his servants with him, and all Israel; and they destroyed the children of Ammon, and besieged Rabbah. But David tarried still at Jerusalem. And it came to pass in an eveningtide, that David arose from off his bed, and walked upon the roof of the king's house: and from the roof he saw a woman washing herself; and the woman was very beautiful to look upon. And David sent and inquired after the woman. And one said, Is not this Bathsheba, the daughter of Eliam, the wife of Uriah the Hittite? And David sent messengers, and took her; and she came in unto him, and he lay with her; for she was purified from her uncleanness: and she returned unto her house. And the woman conceived, and sent and told David, and said, I am with child.*

[4] *"But now thy kingdom shall not continue: the LORD hath sought him a man after his own heart" (I Samuel 13:14a KJV).*

In the Galatians 5:19 - 21 passage, Paul is really warning that it is those who have an ongoing lifestyle of sinful behavior or attitudes that will not inherit the kingdom of God. John put it this way, *"No one who is born of God will continue to sin, because God's seed remains in him; he cannot go on sinning, because he has been born of God" (I John 3:9)*. Yet, we may also conclude that if a person has surrendered to the dominion of a sinful behavior or attitude and has ceased to struggle against it, then at least for the present, he **appears** to fit Paul's description as one who "practices" these things. Therefore, such a man should have no subjective assurance of salvation while he remains "caught in sin" or put another way, "enslaved to sin."

The Apostle Paul taught that Christians are no longer slaves to sin. (See Romans 6:6.[5]) If a Christian is enslaved to sin, it will only be a temporary condition and one that is in contradiction to the new nature. God works to correct the temporary condition. *"It is God who works in you to will and to act according to His good purpose" (Philippians 2:13)*. If the man continues to live a life surrendered to the dominion of a sinful behavior or attitude and God never delivers him out of it through His loving chastening work, then that man would appear to be a bastard, not one of God's children. *"If you are not disciplined (and everyone undergoes discipline), then you are illegitimate children and not true sons" (Hebrews 12:8)*. Thus, Paul's statement is true that all who willfully continue to live under the dominion of a sinful behavior or attitude (practice these things) will not inherit the Kingdom of God; they are not God's children.

II Corinthians 5:17 states, *"If anyone is in Christ, he is a new creation; the old has gone, the new has come!"* Those who are "in Christ" have been born of God. The first epistle of John teaches that all who are born of God have a new nature and that they will walk in the light.

---

[5] *"Knowing this, that our old self was crucified with Him, in order that our body of sin might be done away with, so that we would no longer be slaves to sin" (Romans 6:6 NASB)*.

Their lives will be visibly different than those of unbelievers. (See I John 1:6[6]) It will be as if they are dancing to the beat of a different drum. We must conclude that while it is possible for Christians to commit grossly sinful acts, such acts will not characterize their life. Jesus said that we can recognize whether a person is "in the faith" by the fruit his life produces. (See Matthew 7:20.[7]) While an isolated sinful act or acts might occur, such acts will not characterize the life of a true believer. Therefore, habitual sinful behavior patterns may suggest the absence of a regenerate heart. (It appears that he has not been born again.)

According to Romans 8:5, an unregenerate man has his mind set on the desires of the sinful nature. He is dominated by his sinful nature. He does not have the power of the Spirit to be freed of it. It does not matter whether the habitual sinful behavior involves another person or if it is done in secret (such as self-gratification). If a person remains controlled by it indefinitely, he should question whether he knows the Lord. He must not minimize his addiction by measuring himself against other people who profess to know Christ. He should not think that since the problem is so widespread that somehow the danger of hell is not present. Jesus said, *"Wide is the path and broad is the road that leads to destruction and many enter through it" (Matthew 7:13).* Many who claim to be Christians will find out some day that they never actually knew Christ. (See Matthew 7:22-23.[8]) We must not just chalk our sinful behavior tendencies up to "human weakness." If we remain enslaved to sinful behavior, then there is reason to wonder if the Holy Spirit lives within us (if we are truly regenerate).

---

[6] *If we say that we have fellowship with Him and yet walk in the darkness, we lie and do not practice the truth (I John 1:6 NASB).*

[7] *"Wherefore by their fruits ye shall know them" (Matthew 7:20 KJV).*

[8] *Many on that day will say to me, 'Lord, Lord, did we not prophesy in your name, and cast out demons in your name, and do many mighty works in your name?' And I will declare to them, 'I never knew you; depart from me, you workers of lawlessness' (Matthew 7:22-23).*

What to do if you are a Christian caught in habitual sin.

If you find yourself in this predicament, you are undoubtedly discouraged and wonder if you will ever be able to live free of addiction. You have probably wondered why other Christians don't seem to experience what it is like to fall prey to addiction and assumed that you are simply wired differently. If you are one of these people, I want you to be assured that THERE IS HOPE for you!

The world has labels for people prone to addictions. The world diagnoses the problem and affixes labels like "bipolar," "manic" and other nonsensical terms. In general, the world says that these people have "addictive personalities." While it may appear that such people do indeed have "addictive personalities," such labels tend to ignore the possibility of true, sustained deliverance that God is able to provide. Once a person receives such a label, he often begins to accept the notion that this is simply the way he is wired while other people are wired in such a way that they are not prone to addictions. While it may be true that you are more prone to addictions than certain other people, you must not blindly accept this as your fate in life. The Bible teaches that there is deliverance in Christ!

According to the world, I was one of those people who had an addictive personality. During my life, I have experienced what it is like to be "hopelessly" addicted to drugs and pornography. I can assure you that neither of these things hold me captive now and their pull diminishes more and more as the years pass.

Alcoholics Anonymous teaches that once a person is an alcoholic, he is always an alcoholic. I realize that through this teaching, they are trying to tell people that once they stop drinking, they must always be on guard and recognize that alcohol is dangerous and must be avoided. I agree. But I do not agree with the statement itself. ("Once a person is an alcoholic, he is always an alcoholic.") I believe that God is able to change the very fabric of our being in such a way that our tastes for things change. So, instead of getting a thrill from being buzzed, we find it distasteful and unpleasant. This is the type of change we need for true, sustained deliverance. This is the type of change that God has produced in me. If this were not possible for you, then temptations to do the things that hold you captive would never diminish after you quit the habit. Then, you would eventually succumb to temptation during a future weaker moment. As one who had a hopelessly addictive personality, I hereby testify that God is able to change you and deliver you truly!

God is able to change the very fabric of your being. He is able to "rewire" you. If you want sustained deliverance, you must strive for nothing less and believe that by His power, this can and will be accomplished. This cannot be achieved through self-reformation. Yet, there are indeed steps you must take. But when you are delivered, you will look back on it giving all glory to God and proclaim in your heart, "With God, all things are possible and apart from Him, I can do nothing!" (Whenever God delivers, He gets all the glory in our hearts.)

Acknowledge that you need to be delivered.

If you find yourself engaged in sinful behavior of some sort on a regular basis, you must first realize that you are caught in sin. If you minimize the problem, you won't see a need to deal with it and will never want deliverance badly enough to seek it. If this describes your situation, then you really are not ready to experience deliverance. Perhaps you should reread the beginning portion of this book and ask yourself, "Am I really one of God's children?" God's children **HATE** the bondage of sin. *yes*

Assuming you realize that you are caught in a habitual sin, you still need to become convinced about the true state of your condition. You must be fully convinced in *yes* your heart that you cannot break the grip of the sin that holds you captive. You must be fully convinced in your heart that only God can truly deliver you.

Understand what actually holds you captive.

In case you do not yet understand this, some words need to be said concerning the nature of physical addiction verses emotional addiction. Most people think that physical addiction is the most powerful aspect of addiction to break, not the "mental" aspect of addiction. This is simply not true. While it may be true that the physical aspect of addiction is what drug users fear the most, it is not the physical addiction that truly grips the person. While withdrawal from physical addictions can result in violent physical reactions such as convulsions, vomiting, etc., the physical addiction passes immediately after the physical withdrawal is complete. If the physical aspect of addiction was the most gripping aspect, then heroin addicts would be free of their addictions immediately after the physical withdrawal phase. But statistics show that most of them fall back into heroin addiction again and again after they withdraw from their physical addiction. It is the emotional aspect of addiction that really holds long term sway over addicts. So, even though marijuana is not physically addicting, it is still highly addictive, just like heroin. Because the real problem relates to emotional attachment, anything that is pleasurable to the flesh is highly addictive. So, heroin, marijuana, alcohol, uppers, downers, pornography, and yes, even food and non-alcoholic beverages are all highly addictive.

Begin taking steps that will play a role in God rewiring you.

If you are truly a Christian, you can have deliverance but you must first want it. The degree to which you want deliverance will be reflected by your willingness to apply yourself to the things God has said. If you find yourself wavering, it is only because your desire for deliverance is less than it needs to be. If you end up faltering, not all is lost. God can use even your failure. He can use it to produce even greater desire for deliverance. Keep looking to Him and eventually, He will lift you out of the miry clay and set you firmly on the Rock.

Your desire for deliverance will be reflected by your willingness to take the steps that the Bible prescribes. You cannot sit passively by and expect God to simply zap you with a powerful deliverance. This is going to take emotionally draining effort on your part. Your flesh has been conditioned to take comfort from the sins that have held you in bondage. Fighting this requires that you leave that comfort and opt for that steep walk up the mountain. Along the way, sometimes you will want to stop and take comfort in the old way of living. Your emotions will weigh heavily on you. In your own power, you have no chance to gain the victory, even over your own emotions. But because you are a believer, you can keep casting yourself upon God and draw upon the refreshment that comes from being in His presence. As you embark upon this steep climb, take heed to one of God's oft used exhortations, "Be courageous." When your emotions are telling you to retreat, be courageous and shrug them off. The unbeliever has no reason to believe this will do any good. But because God is with you, you have every reason to be courageous and believe that deliverance is up ahead.

Before you begin, you must plan now to be in it for the long run. Though God could make deliverance seem almost instantaneous, plan for it to take time. Remember, a sustained deliverance requires that you be changed from within. In other words, you need to be rewired so that your likes and dislikes change. At this point, you may enjoy being encouraged by the Bible and other Christians. But you also like being comforted by your sin. (Your flesh likes it.) Your enjoyment of wholesome things must increase and your like of unwholesome things must decrease. It might be hard for you to imagine that this is even possible. Yet, this is what the Bible prescribes and millions of Christians have experienced it. If you are a believer, your enjoyment of wholesome things WILL INCREASE as long as you feed that wholesome side of your appetite. As you do, your desire for unwholesome things WILL DECREASE. But you must be willing to feed that wholesome side of your appetite. According to the Apostle Paul, If we walk in the Spirit, we will not fulfill the lusts of the flesh. (See Galatians 5:16). So, assuming you seriously want deliverance, consider some practical things you should do to feed the wholesome side of your appetite.

Begin rehearsing the things God has said concerning your situation.

Perhaps you should write out a few of the things God has said and keep them posted in your house. Then, you can review them often. Below are just a few of them:

> *Knowing this, that our old man is crucified with him, that the body of sin might be destroyed, that henceforth we should not serve sin. (Romans 6:6 KJV).*

> *Ask, and it shall be given you; seek, and ye shall find; knock, and it shall be opened unto you (Matthew 7:7KJV).*

> *I am crucified with Christ: nevertheless I live; yet not I, but Christ liveth in me: and the life which I now live in the flesh I live by the faith of the Son of God, who loved me, and gave himself for me (Galatians 2:20 KJV).*

> *There hath no temptation taken you but such as is common to man: but God is faithful, who will not suffer you to be tempted above that ye are able; but will with the temptation also make a way to escape, that ye may be able to bear it (I Corinthians 10:13 KJV).*

> *If God be for us, who can be against us? He that spared not his own Son, but delivered him up for us all, how shall he not with him also freely give us all things? (Romans 8:31b & 32 KJV).*

I realize that many of these things may seem unattainable or foreign to your experience right now, but don't let that stop you from disciplining yourself to rehearse them. Over time, they will take root if you are diligent to meditate on them. Your flesh wants nothing to do with them. But God is able to make them impart life to your spirit. You must want deliverance bad enough to do these basic things.

Pray.

No matter where you find yourself, you can and should always pray. If you apply yourself to gain deliverance, know for certain that God is aware of your struggle. The fact that you are trying to gain deliverance is something He is happy about. He is on your side. (See Romans 8:31-32.[9]) He also knows that it is very difficult for you. He is rooting for you. But more than that, He is right by your side helping you, even if it does not seem so at times.

Knowing that God is near to the weak and brokenhearted, you should take courage in your praying and know that He is listening with all attention. (See Psalms 34:18[10].) He wants to show you His great love and power. But He wants you to learn endurance in the process of being delivered. Remember that Jesus said, "Seek and you shall find."

---

[9] *If God be for us, who can be against us? He that spared not his own Son, but delivered him up for us all, how shall he not with him also freely give us all things? (Romans 8:31b & 32 KJV).*

[10] *The LORD is near to the brokenhearted and saves those who are crushed in spirit (Psalm 34:18 NASB).*

Fellowship with true believers in a local church where Jesus is Lord.

Though God can deliver under any means, you would be a fool to expect deliverance if you isolate yourself from other believers. As you most likely already have discovered, unwholesome friends pull you down into unwholesome living patterns. (See I Corinthians 15:33.[11]) And if the bond with those friends is strong, the bond to those unwholesome living patterns will be stronger than if those people were not in your life. Similarly, wholesome friends can, and normally will, have the opposite effect on your life. But unfortunately, we must first define the nature of wholesome friends that are necessary. While it might be helpful to have friends that are not drug users, it would be much, much better to have friends that have a deep relationship with God and are able by their lives and words to help you spiritually, not just emotionally. Imagine how helpful it would be to hang around with Jesus while you are on your path toward deliverance.

---

[11] "Do not be deceived: "Bad company corrupts good morals" (I Corinthians 15:33 NASB).

[12] "Take heed, brethren, lest there be in any of you an evil heart of unbelief, in departing from the living God. But exhort one another daily, while it is called To day; lest any of you be hardened through the deceitfulness of sin" (Hebrews 3:12-13 KJV).

There are many people on earth who claim to be Christian. Not all of these people will be of help to you during your time of struggle. In fact, some of them might actually have a detrimental effect. But if you could hang around with people who truly know Jesus and walk by faith, then you have an opportunity to form bonds with people who are also fighting the fight. (See Hebrews 3:12-13.[12]) They may not have been addicted to the same things you have been addicted to, but they do possess that same unruly flesh that is bent in the same direction as your flesh. If they are walking by faith, they have to deny the flesh in the same way you have to deny your flesh. Like you, they also stumble and have to get back up. So, assuming they are genuine and not living a fake Christian life, you will find that you have a common bond.

Together, you are treading the pathway of faith with all its suffering and trials. If you have relationships of this nature with true Christians, the grace of God has opportunity to flow freely and abundantly into your life giving you great advantage in this battle.

In today's lukewarm setting, it might be difficult to find other Christians who live without pretense. (Christians that pretend to be spiritually minded so that their Christian friends will look up to them are people who live with pretense.) Any pretense strangles the flow of God's grace in the lives of God's people. Ask God to help you find spiritually strong Christians who are living without pretense. Hopefully, you will be able to form relationships with one or more Christians who are open and live without pretense.

You must have a goal of being in Christian relationships in which you can be honest about your situation. But if, in your Christian relationships, you act as if nothing is wrong in front of your fellow believers, you will be acting as a hypocrite and God's grace to deliver will be choked off. Hypocrisy is a gross sin of pride and the Bible clearly states, *"God resists the proud but gives grace to the humble" (James 4:6 KJV).*

It is foolish to expect God to deliver if you are not willing to humble yourself in the eyes of men. Just as Naaman could not be healed unless he dunked himself seven times in the Jordan River, neither will you be healed unless you discard your hypocrisy. (See II Kings 4:1-14.) But if we "humble ourselves before the Lord, He will lift us up" (James 4:10). If you are blessed to enjoy relationships with Christians in which there is no pretense, then you will be able to take advantage further by requesting prayer. James says, *"Confess your sins to each other and pray for each other so that you may be healed" (James 5:16 KJV).* If you are a believer, you should recognize how great an advantage it would be if more of God's people were praying for you at this crucial time. On the contrary, if nobody knows about your need of deliverance, nobody will pray for you.

As already mentioned, God is opposed to the proud and gives grace to the humble. If you are aware of something you did to someone in the past that you have not made right, you must not expect the grace of God to flow in your life. (See Matthew 5:23-24.[13]) If you stole something that you have not repaid or if you have not confessed your sin to somebody that you defrauded, you must make things right before expecting deliverance. Any hidden sin of this nature is a roadblock to deliverance. You might not have the resources to make it fully right. But you must start by confessing your sin to the one you wronged and pledge that you will make it right even if you don't have the resources to do so immediately. If you fail to do this, you demonstrate that you really do not want deliverance from the sins that hold you in bondage badly enough. Any unresolved issues of this nature represent strongholds that keep you enslaved in many other sins. They are all connected and must be broken.

It should be noted also that less flagrant sins also represent road blocks to deliverance. For example, if you verbally attacked somebody, you must confess to them that you were wrong and ask them to forgive you. In other words, you must make things right in your relationships damaged by your sin. You may need to confess sins you committed against a friend or spouse (to them). If you try to live with hidden sins, you will not find deliverance from habitual sin.

---

[13] *"Therefore if thou bring thy gift to the altar, and there rememberest that thy brother hath ought against thee; Leave there thy gift before the altar, and go thy way; first be reconciled to thy brother, and then come and offer thy gift"* (Matthew 5:23-24 KJV).

Be transformed by the renewing of your mind.

In Ephesians 5:26, the Apostle Paul alludes to the power of God's Word to wash and clean. In Romans 12:2 he speaks of being transformed by the renewing of our minds. Earlier, I used the analogy of being rewired to demonstrate the nature of the changes that God is able to bring about in us. If a man quits a habit while nothing is done to change his appetite, he will most likely gravitate back into that habit. But if he is changed within so that his tastes are changed, he will begin to find that old sin distasteful and undesirable. This is what is required for a sustained deliverance.

When a person is caught in sin, their taste for the Bible is usually diminished and he pays less attention to it. But to have sustained deliverance, that person must not neglect the Bible. Otherwise, the great transforming work that God desires to do will be woefully hindered. Satan wants you to be held fast in sin. He will do things to distract you from the Bible. But that age-old principle, garbage in, garbage out will be on display if you neglect the Bible. God's grace comes to us in a variety of ways. I have already mentioned two important ones, prayer and fellowship with true believers. Likewise, the Bible is a substantial means of grace that is essential to the rewiring God wants to do in your life. He offers to do the rewiring but you must make yourself available for the work. If you fail to give your attention to the Bible, don't expect to experience the rewiring that is necessary to bring about sustained deliverance.

So what can you do to put yourself under this shower of grace? You can read your Bible daily. You can memorize truth relating to God's deliverance work. You can study the Bible by yourself and with other Christians. But above all, you must learn to <u>live</u> the Bible. Only as it is being lived will the rewiring take place. What do I mean by living the Bible? When your faith is put to the test and you are made uncomfortable, you are put in a position where you must choose how you will respond. If you retreat and take comfort in worldly things that give the flesh pleasure, you will miss the grace God intends to give. But if you wait upon God and call upon Him to help you without retreating, that grace of God is unleashed in you causing you to undergo transformation. You are making a conscious choice to believe and obey what the Bible says, even while under temptation to retreat. Through all this, you are being rewired <u>by God's grace</u>. It might not seem like it at the time, but the grace of God is flowing. As long as you continue drawing upon Him this way for help, believing and obeying His Word, you will be transformed inside. In time, you will notice your tastes changing. You will appreciate wholesome things from God much more and you will begin to see the horribleness of your old way of living. This takes time. So again, you must be in it for the long haul. But do so expecting results because I assure you, they will come if you are a Christian!

Do God's will as one who is advancing His Kingdom.

If you are in need of deliverance from a habitual sin, you need a complete change in your thinking, attitudes and behavior. The changes of attitudes and behavior are the most difficult. Changes in thinking are the least painful but unless you are at least willing to open yourself up to the idea that your entire view of Christianity has been distorted up until now, you will fail to lay hold of God's grace necessary for the changes that need to take place in your attitudes and behaviors. If you are willing, then please consider the following words.

In many ways, the church has departed from the New Testament model and has adopted a distorted understanding of what the church is supposed to be like and how we are to thrive as Christians. Typically, Christians have adopted the unbiblical clergy/laity mentality. Jesus and His Apostles taught that the leadership was never intended to do the work of the ministry. Instead, they are to equip **the saints (us) to do the work of the ministry**. Leaders are supposed to lead by example and that leading is intended to produce ministers, not mere spectators who attend church services. When the saints (us) have been properly equipped and are engaged in the mission God has purposed for them individually, the gospel permeates the world around us. (See I Thessalonians 1:4-2:14.) In other words, the ministry impacts the world around us. If this is not happening in the lives of the members of any given church, biblical Christianity is not on display there. Also, the Bible teaches that this type of ministry is a spontaneous outcome of the Holy Spirit's work, not one motivated by a paycheck.

Biblical Christianity is incredibly radical compared to what is on display today in North America. If you truly want deliverance, you must come to grips with the fact that you must jettison your current view of Christianity and fix your eyes on the Biblical pattern of Christian living. In other words, you must embrace the fact that you can no longer settle for the typical pattern of Christianity. If you want deliverance, you must accept the fact that your entire life must change radically. You can no longer live as a mere spectator. You have to be different than most, if not every Christian you know.

You must reject the false notion that ministry is for the "professionals." God has a special ministry in mind for you. The outcome of that ministry is restricted only by the extent you are willing to pursue it. It should not be considered a token ministry (something you do on the side). It must be a main part of your life. You need to realize that God may want to save millions of people using you.

If you think that you do not possess the spiritual abilities to be used in such a big way, let me call your attention to Joni Erikson Tada. She suffered a spinal injury as a teenager and unbeliever and has been a quadriplegic for many years. God saved her and she began to ask Him what He wanted her to do. God guided her to do many things and has used her to save many, many people all around the world. If God can use a quadriplegic to accomplish great things, He can accomplish mighty things through you. You must begin to accept your identity as a minister of God and believe He wants to accomplish mighty things through you personally.

The Bible teaches us what God desires for us to be and to do. As we learn what He wants us to do, we must begin to do it. Otherwise, we will delude ourselves and transformation and deliverance will remain out of reach. But imagine waking up each day and knowing exactly what God wants you to do that day. Then imagine doing it, knowing that you are fulfilling God's express purpose for you that day. Now imagine also that doing these things brings you joy, satisfaction and peace. Such a way of life makes the soul fat. When the soul is fed with this type of food, the smell and taste of garbage offered by the world is less and less appealing.

Just over twenty years ago, I wandered from the path and began eating from the dumpster this world offers. When God mercifully turned me back to walk in the path of righteousness, I was spiritually weak and prone to stumble. But as His grace came to me through the same means mentioned above, I gained more and more strength. But I was still spiritually weak. Then, I sensed God calling me to engage in regular evangelism. By His grace, I embarked on a weekly ministry of door to door evangelism. After doing this for about two years, I began to sense a certain spiritual strength that I had not experienced before in my prior twenty years as a Christian. There was a heightened sense of urgency and alertness about the spiritual war to which God has called us. I mentioned this to my friend who also had been doing this evangelistic work and he noticed the very same thing in his life.

Suddenly, John 4:34 made clear sense to me like never before. After doing the work of evangelism with the woman at the well, Jesus' disciples showed up with food. Jesus told them that He had food that they did not know about. The disciples wondered where Jesus got the food. Then Jesus said, *"My food is to do the will of the Father."* Truly, doing God's will is necessary food for our soul. Without it, we will remain feeble and sustained deliverance will be in question. But eating this food (doing His will) drastically brings about renewal and makes us full of life. We will be made fat by the Bread of Heaven as we do God's will. The things of earth will become strange food that only satisfies earth dwellers.

Always get back up after you stumble.

Though it is possible that God keeps you from ever stumbling in your battle against habitual sin, most will stumble multiple times during the process. The fact that you stumble does not prove you are an unbeliever. It is how a person responds after stumbling that matters. A believer believes that God is truly able to deliver him even though at the moment, he has not yet been delivered. Because he believes that God is able to deliver, he gets back up after he stumbles with an even greater disgust for his sin and desire for deliverance. He gets back up because, in spite of stumbling, he has hope of deliverance.

If you stumble, not all is lost. Remember that God has been and still is making progress in you even though you just stumbled. He even uses your stumbling in the process of changing you from within. If you sailed through the process, you might inwardly think that you simply quit the habitual sin, no big deal. But because you stumbled (and perhaps multiple times) during the process, you truly believe in your heart that it was indeed God who delivered. You believe more than ever that without Jesus, you can do nothing. In other words, God uses this process to bring about true humility in you. After being delivered, you will be able to relate to all people, whether they are kings or homeless vagabonds. You will not see yourself as if you are better than other people, just because you live righteously. You will always remember that unless God keeps you, you will be right back in the dumpster satisfied with garbage instead of feasting on the Bread of Heaven.

Regain assurance of your salvation.

If you stumble, it is important to remember that your experience is no different than any other Christian. Though they may not have been caught in the same sin, every Christian has experienced the battle against sin. Every Christian has stumbled while in that battle, including the Apostle Paul. (See Romans 7:13-25.) When we stumble, we might wonder if we are truly regenerate. You might ask yourself, "Am I saved? After all, I keep stumbling and most of my Christian friends don't seem to struggle the way I struggle."

This is actually a logical question. The subjective assurance of salvation is not based on a one-time decision you made in your past. You can't gain subjective assurance by remembering when you walked down an aisle to receive Jesus or asked Him into your heart. You can't gain subjective assurance by looking back on some emotional experience you had in your past that you assume was your conversion. None of these can produce subjective assurance of salvation. (In themselves these things provide no evidence of true conversion.) Subjective assurance is produced only as we walk with Jesus daily and see the fruit of the Holy Spirit bubbling up in our lives. (See Galatians 5:22-23.[14]) A person can go to church for years thinking he is a Christian simply because he believes all the right things and belongs to a church where everyone considers him to be a believer. This is not the basis for subjective assurance. A person can falsely think he is a Christian. Unless he sees fruit that only God's Spirit can produce flowing from him, he has no real evidence that indicates he is a Christian.

---

[14] *The fruit of the Spirit is love, joy, peace, patience, kindness, goodness, faithfulness, gentleness, self-control; against such things there is no law. (Galatians 5:22-23 NASB).*

So, if you are caught in habitual sin, you probably have very little subjective assurance. At best, you can look back on your life as a follower of Jesus and identify times during which there seemed to be genuine fruit of the Holy Spirit flowing in your life. But because of your current situation, you are left wondering if you are a Christian at all. If a person is caught in habitual sin and he has not wondered this, he is probably not a Christian.

True believers have a strong concern about their salvation because they truly believe what the Bible says about the coming judgment and they do not want to hear Jesus say on that day, *"Depart from me, I never knew you."* (See Matthew 7:22-23). So, if you are concerned, that is actually a good sign that you are a believer. It is people who falsely assume they are Christians who will be surprised on judgment day.

During times when subjective assurance of salvation is low or absent, what should a believer do? The Bible tells us the appropriate response. In the sixth chapter of the Gospel of John, Jesus was teaching some things that seemed absurd to most of the people listening. Many of the people in the narrative are called disciples of Jesus. He told them that unless a man eats His body and drinks His blood, he does not abide in Jesus. When most of these disciples heard these things, they said, *"Who can listen to this?"* Then they stopped following Jesus. Jesus' words became a test of their faith and by leaving, these people proved that they were false disciples. Then He turned to the twelve and asked, *"What about you. Are you going to leave also?"* Peter replied, *"Where can we go? You have the words of eternal life."* This statement helps us see into Peter's heart and there we find that faith was alive and well.

If you have been born again, you can identify with Peter's response. If your subjective assurance is low or absent, you must take your eyes off of your current failures and turn them back on Jesus. Right now, in the midst of your struggle, let your heart cry out to Jesus, *"I have no where else to go Jesus. You have the words of eternal life."* The Apostle Paul tells us that this is precisely what he did when struggling. Instead of focusing on his current or past struggles or victories he said, *"Oh that I may know Him and the power of His resurrection and the fellowship of His sufferings, being conformed to His death; in order that I may attain to the resurrection from the dead. Not that I have already obtained it or have already become perfect, but I press on so that I may lay hold of that for which also I was laid hold of by Christ Jesus. Brethren, I do not regard myself as having laid hold of it yet; but one thing I do: forgetting what lies behind and reaching forward to what lies ahead, I press on toward the goal for the prize of the upward call of God in Christ Jesus"* (Philippians 3:10-14 NASB).

Nail all your guilt to the cross.

You must discipline yourself to reject Satan's accusations. He loves to abuse Christians and one of his chief methods is to whisper accusations into their ears. He will tell you that you are pathetic. He might tell you that you are not a Christian. He especially likes to heap guilt upon you if you let him. If you ever find yourself wallowing in guilt over your sins against God, you need to bring all that guilt right to the cross. Jesus paid in full for your sins. If you do not believe that, then you are essentially saying that Jesus' work was insufficient. Jesus paid it all! His death has brought full reconciliation. He bore all of God's wrath on the cross. The Bible says that we are to come boldly to the throne of grace,[15] not wallow in guilt.

So, if Satan whispers accusations in your ear, you can agree with him when he says that you are pathetic. We all are pathetic. But if he tries to heap guilt on you for your sins against God, you can confess to God that you have indeed sinned. But do not accept Satan's temptation to wallow in guilt because Jesus bore all your sins on the cross and as a result, you are "accepted in the Beloved." Tell God that you are clinging to the cross and thank Him that Jesus died to bear all your sins.[16]

---

[15] *Therefore let us draw near with confidence to the throne of grace, so that we may receive mercy and find grace to help in time of need (Hebrews 4:16 NASB).*

[16] It should be noted that in contrast to Satan's work of accusing us to ourselves, the Holy Spirit is working to bring about a healthy conviction of sin. (See John 16 and Psalm 139:23-24). We can discern the difference. Satan accuses us to cause us to hide from God and wallow in self-pity, and give up. The Spirit's conviction leads to agreement with God that our action or attitude is sinful, repentance from our sin toward our holy Father, casting ourselves upon his mercy displayed in the cross, awareness of our inability to earn God's pleasure by an act of the will, and seeking his power and presence to obey in the future.

Realize the stakes if you fail to obtain deliverance.

We are powerless in our own strength to deliver ourselves. (See Romans 8:5-8.[17]) But God is fully able to deliver us and He delights to show His glory by delivering us out of bondage. Sometimes Christians find themselves caught in sinful traps that seem impossible to break. It is as if their backs are to the sea and they have nowhere to go. (See Exodus 14:9-10.[18])

At times like this we must desperately seek God for supernatural deliverance. In these situations, everything is on the line. If I cannot find deliverance by God's power, I am at a spiritual impasse. There is no moving forward. Also, the power of God is in question. If He cannot work this power in me, then logic suggests that either I am not His child[19] or He is not the almighty God (and we know that the latter is not in question). This is why it is a desperate situation requiring desperate pleading with faith toward God.

[17] *"They that are after the flesh do mind the things of the flesh; but they that are after the Spirit the things of the Spirit. For to be carnally minded is death; but to be spiritually minded is life and peace. Because the carnal mind is enmity against God: for it is not subject to the law of God, neither indeed can be. So then they that are in the flesh cannot please God" (Romans 8:5-8 KJV).*

[18] *"But the Egyptians pursued after them, all the horses and chariots of Pharaoh, and his horsemen, and his army, and overtook them encamping by the sea, beside Pihahiroth, before Baalzephon. And when Pharaoh drew nigh, the children of Israel lifted up their eyes, and, behold, the Egyptians marched after them; and they were sore afraid: and the children of Israel cried out unto the LORD" (Exodus 14:9-10 KJV).*

[19] If a person is a new creature in Christ, he is just that, a new creature. He desires to enjoy God and when he can't, he is miserable. He sees all sin as a destructive force that blinds him from God's glory. He pleads with God to grant him a heart of faithful obedience rooted in trust of his loving Father. He cannot live as unregenerate people do who disobey without blinking an eye. The unregenerate man would rather go with the flow and sin as long as his sin does not find him out. The Christian does not refrain from sin just for fear of getting caught. He knows he is caught the moment he sins because he senses misery and destruction in his heart. His view of God's glory is diminished and he begins confessing it to God and clinging to the cross. So, it is a matter of how a person relates to these sins. The unregenerate person relates one way to them and the regenerate relates in quite a different way.

This desperation should drive us to take desperate measures.[20] If our faith is genuine, it will cause us to continue seeking deliverance until God delivers. Only unbelievers can be content to continue walking on the wide road that leads to destruction. This means that if we stumble, we get back up and seek God's deliverance over and over continually. God uses such struggling to humble us and magnify His power as the great Deliverer. If we cease to get back up and resign to live under the slavery of sin, we have no assurance of gaining eternal life. When God does deliver us, He is most magnified. When supernatural deliverance takes place, it is obvious to the one delivered that it was God who brought it about. It is like the moving of a mountain! It also produces humility to go through such a trial. We did all that we could but were unable to deliver ourselves. We finally came to the place where we agreed with God that we were helpless and we desperately sought His help. It was God alone that delivered us. The experience makes us all the more cautious about the dangers of that which previously entrapped us. We plead with God to keep us near Him so that we do not fall prey to the enemy.

---

[20] Besides the measures already mentioned, you should also consider other steps. For example, you should not go places where you would likely be tempted and avoid old friends that are caught in the same habitual sin. Depending on your situation, you might also eliminate the use of computers and other entertainment or communication devices all in an effort to do "whatever it takes" to battle the sin that plagues you.

Avoid snares that lie ahead.

If we are not presently caught in the bondage of sinful behavior patterns, we are free to enjoy God without the hindrance of such sins. To avoid being trapped by Satan's snares, we must walk close to the Shepherd of our soul. To do this, we must walk humbly before Him with hearts of faithful obedience believing that we are capable of any sin and kept by God alone. If we do not walk humbly in faithful obedience, we take ourselves out of God's protection and make ourselves susceptible to Satan's attacks. *"Be of sober spirit, be on the alert. Your adversary, the devil, prowls about like a roaring lion, seeking someone to devour" (I Peter 5:8 NASB).* This is an all or nothing principle. If there is any disobedience or attitudes of self-sufficiency in our lives, there will be chinks in our God-given armor. God's protection is found in His presence with a heart of dependence on Him alone. God promised, if we, *"Walk in the Spirit, we will not fulfill the lusts of the flesh" (Galatians 5:16 KJV).* When we are walking close with Him, our souls are made fat by the Heavenly Manna. When our souls have been feasting on Jesus, we are satisfied with the true Bread of Life. When we are enjoying this Manna, the counterfeit food from the world does not have the same level of attraction. It is more easily recognized for what it is - garbage that can only make us sick and rob us of the enjoyment of God's glory.

When we are savoring the Manna, we see the crucial need to "put to death[21] whatever belongs to our earthly nature: sexual immorality, impurity, lust, evil desires and greed, which is idolatry." (See Colossians 3:5.) We are taught also that in order to walk close with Him, in obedience, we must be engaged in the mission He has given to His church. Each of us has been given spiritual gifts by God for the building up of the Body of Christ.

---

[21] *The indicative of faith must be matched by the imperative of ethics" (p. 203). The verb nekrosate, meaning literally "to make dead," is very strong. It suggests that we are not simply to suppress or control evil acts and attitudes. We are to wipe them out, completely exterminate the old way of life. "Slay utterly" may*

If we are not engaged fully from the heart in the work He planned for us to do, we will be like King David who stayed back at the palace while his army went to war. His lazy attitude made him susceptible to temptation and he succumbed to it. (See II Samuel 11:1-4.[22])

If we choose to be entertained by the court jesters in the comfort of the palace, we will become spiritually lazy. We must be engaged in the battle or we will be prone to Satan's traps. For more insight concerning the spiritual war and how to prepare yourself for it, I recommend my book, **Overcoming the Powers of Darkness - Using God's Spiritual Armor**, *described in the "Other Books by Tom Bear" Section near the back of this book.*

---

express its force. The form of the verb (aorist imperative) makes clear that the action is to be undertaken decisively, with a sense of urgency. Both the meaning of the verb and the force of the tense suggest a vigorous, painful act of personal determination. Maclaren likens it to a man who while working at a machine gets his fingers drawn between rollers or caught in the belting. "Another minute and he will be flattened to a shapeless bloody mass. He catches up an axe lying by and with his own arm hacks off his own hand at the wrist.... It is not easy nor pleasant, but it is the only alternative to a horrible death" (p. 275). NIV Commentary Col 3:5ff*B*

[22] *"It came to pass, after the year was expired, at the time when kings go forth to battle, that David sent Joab, and his servants with him, and all Israel; and they destroyed the children of Ammon, and besieged Rabbah. But David tarried still at Jerusalem. And it came to pass in an eveningtide, that David arose from off his bed, and walked upon the roof of the king's house: and from the roof he saw a woman washing herself; and the woman was very beautiful to look upon. And David sent and inquired after the woman. And one said, Is not this Bathsheba, the daughter of Eliam, the wife of Uriah the Hittite? And David sent messengers, and took her; and she came in unto him, and he lay with her; for she was purified from her uncleanness: and she returned unto her house" (II Samuel 11:1-4 KJV).*

In summary, if we are caught in sinful behavior, we should question whether we really know Jesus. If we find ourselves trapped by sin, we must persistently plead with God for supernatural deliverance and begin taking steps that facilitate deliverance. If we are currently free from it, we must walk humbly each day in God's presence, satisfying ourselves in Him alone. We must watch over our hearts with all diligence (Proverbs 4:23.[23]) knowing that except for God's grace, we will fall. *"Let him who thinks he stands take heed lest he fall" (I Corinthians 10:12 NASB).* May God purify His people so that His light shines brightly in us!

Note concerning "accountability groups:" Some people teach that you should join an accountability group. The idea is that the people in the group share a common struggle with some type of addiction. They intentionally meet on a regular basis and tell if they have remained free of their sin since the last meeting. One of the supposed potential benefits is that members are motivated to stay clean so they can give a good report to the group. While there may be some things a group can provide, coerced accountability is not the answer. Our motivation to be free must not be based upon trying to maintain an appearance of deliverance in the eyes of people in an accountability group. This is artificial deliverance.

---

[23] Watch *over your heart with all diligence, for from it flow the springs of life (Proverbs 4:23 NASB).*

Appendix: The Gospel of Jesus Christ

The main content of this book is directed to Christians. Unfortunately, many people are under the false impression that they are Christians when in reality, they aren't. This appendix explains the gospel of Jesus Christ that must be believed from the heart. If you do not believe the gospel as explained here, then you must first come to grips with the fact that you are not truly a Christian. Unless you are a Christian, you must not expect to find sustained deliverance from habitual sin. (All non-Christians remain dead spiritually and unable to free themselves from the slavery of sin.) (See Ephesians 2:1-3.[24]) So, for the sake of your eternal wellbeing, I strongly urge you to read and believe the gospel of Jesus Christ from your heart.

You must come to God His way, not yours.

The only people who are candidates for the salvation Jesus came to provide are people who come to Him on His terms. (See John 14:6.[25]). To be saved, you must discard any thoughts you might have about yourself and God if they are in conflict with what He has said.

---

[24] And you were dead in your trespasses and sins, in which you formerly walked according to the course of this world, according to the prince of the power of the air, of the spirit that is now working in the sons of disobedience. Among them we too all formerly lived in the lusts of our flesh, indulging the desires of the flesh and of the mind, and were by nature children of wrath, even as the rest (Ephesians 2:1-3 NASB).

[25] Jesus said to him, "I am the way, and the truth, and the life; no one comes to the Father but through Me (John 14:6 NASB).

God deserves perfect obedience from us.

God created us and therefore, He owns us. He has graciously provided food, water, covering and even air to breathe. Because He owns us, He has the right to demand perfect obedience from us. We do not have the right to demand anything from Him. The Bible says He is righteous. Another word that can be used to describe Him is fair. He never does anything unjust. Being His lowly creatures, we have no right to accuse Him of being unjust, no matter what we might think.

All people have failed to give God the obedience He deserves.

All people have sinned (broken God's laws) and are guilty. (See Romans 3:10-20.[26]) The Bible teaches that all people DESERVE to go to hell forever for our crimes against God. We cannot erase our sins or make up for them by trying to do good works. (See Isaiah 64:6.[27]) God cannot simply grant a pardon because that would violate His perfect justice.

---

[26] *"There is none righteous, not even one; There is none who understands, There is none who seeks for God; All have turned aside, together they have become useless; There is none who does good, There is not even one." "Their throat is an open grave, With their tongues they keep deceiving," "The poison of asps is under their lips"; "Whose mouth is full of cursing and bitterness"; "Their feet are swift to shed blood, Destruction and misery are in their paths, And the Path of peace they have not known." "There is no fear of God before their eyes." Now we know that whatever the Law says, it speaks to those who are under the Law, so that every mouth may be closed and all the world may become accountable to God; because by the works of the Law no flesh will be justified in His sight; for through the Law comes the knowledge of sin (Romans 3:10-20 NASB)*

[27] *For all of us have become like one who is unclean, and all our righteous deeds are like a filthy garment (Isaiah 64:6a NASB).*

God is absolute in His righteousness

According to the Bible, God's justice is absolute. Even though He is inclined toward mercy, He must punish each and every sin to uphold justice. (See Habakkuk 1:13.[28]) To provide clarity on this issue, the following statement is given: *"If a person lived his entire life without sinning except for one small lie and then died with just that one lie on his account, God would have no choice but to send him to hell forever."* This statement may seem unbelievable to some people, but it is absolutely true. God's perfect justice prohibits Him from excusing any sin. It all must be punished. If you die with any sin whatsoever on your account, you will be cast into hell forever.

---

[28] *Your eyes are too pure to approve evil, and You cannot look on wickedness with favor (Habakkuk 1:13a NASB).*

Because God is merciful, He made a way to save us without compromising His absolute righteousness. (See Romans 3:21-26.[29])

From the beginning, God has been communicating through His prophets His plan to redeem sinners. In order to save sinners, He would provide a substitute sacrifice for sins. He planned to send His divine Son into the world to die in our place. Jesus Christ was born of a virgin. He was without sin. He lived His entire life without ever sinning. This qualified Him to be the substitute sacrifice that God would accept. When He died on the cross, He paid the debt that we could never pay. God then raised Him from the dead indicating that God received this death as payment in full for sins.

---

[29] *But now apart from the Law the righteousness of God has been manifested, being witnessed by the Law and the Prophets, even the righteousness of God through faith in Jesus Christ for all those who believe; for there is no distinction; for all have sinned and fall short of the glory of God, being justified as a gift by His grace through the redemption which is in Christ Jesus; whom God displayed publicly as a propitiation in His blood through faith. This was to demonstrate His righteousness, because in the forbearance of God He passed over the sins previously committed; for the demonstration, I say, of His righteousness at the present time, so that He would be just and the justifier of the one who has faith in Jesus (Romans 3:21-26).*

Salvation is offered to all who believe these things from the heart. (See John 3:16.[30])

If any man believes from the heart that Jesus died for their sins in this way and rose from the dead, they receive remission of sins and eternal life. (See Acts 13:38-39.[31]) The only requirement is that they be sinners and not people who think they are already acceptable to God. In other words, they must recognize that they have rebelled against God and fully deserve God's wrath (hell). (See Luke 18:9-14.[32]) Only people who truly believe this will come to God humbly and look to Him for mercy. Believing these things, they know that they are hopelessly lost and unable to save themselves.

---

[30] *God so loved the world, that He gave His only begotten Son, that <u>whosoever</u> believes in Him shall not perish, but have eternal life (John 3:16 NASB).*

[31] *Therefore let it be known to you, brethren, that through Him forgiveness of sins is proclaimed to you, and through Him everyone who believes is freed from all things, from which you could not be freed through the Law of Moses (Acts 13:38-39 NASB).*

[32] *And He also told this parable to some people who trusted in themselves that they were righteous, and viewed others with contempt: "Two men went up into the temple to pray, one a Pharisee and the other a tax collector. "The Pharisee stood and was praying this to himself: 'God, I thank You that I am not like other people: swindlers, unjust, adulterers, or even like this tax collector. 'I fast twice a week; I pay tithes of all that I get.' "But the tax collector, standing some distance away, was even unwilling to lift up his eyes to heaven, but was beating his breast, saying, 'God, be merciful to me, the sinner!' "I tell you, this man went to his house justified rather than the other; for everyone who exalts himself will be humbled, but he who humbles himself will be exalted" (Luke 18:9-14)*

Jesus died not just to deliver us from the penalty of sin. He came also to deliver us from slavery to it.

To come to God His way, we must begin relating to Jesus as Lord over our lives. This involves the idea of repentance. You must therefore recognize that prior to coming to Him, you lived your life as if you were God, ruling over your own life. Only God has the right to rule over it. But you sought to please yourself and pursue pleasure on your terms rather than live in subjection to His rule.

All who believe the gospel of Jesus Christ from the heart have been raised from spiritual death to new life. (See Ephesians 2:4-5.[33]) They have been changed inside by God's grace so that they no longer resist God. Instead of enjoying sin, they seek to be freed from it. They seek to please God rather than themselves. Furthermore, God begins transforming their lives so that they begin to think and act more and more like Jesus. They become compassionate people. They begin to live holy lives. They find that their old way of living gives way to a life of obedience. They begin enjoying a deep relationship with God, free from the guilt and slavery of sin.

---

[33] *But God, being rich in mercy, because of His great love with which He loved us, even when we were dead in our transgressions, made us alive together with Christ (Ephesians 2:4-5 NASB).*

All who receive the gift of salvation lose their lives to Jesus. (You must count the cost.)

Jesus said, *"Whoever seeks to save his life will lose it, and whoever loses his life will preserve it" (Luke 17:33)*. He also said, *"Whoever does not bear his cross and come after Me cannot be My disciple" (Luke 14:27)*. In other words, unless a person is willing to die for Jesus, he cannot be His disciple. People do not want to give up ownership of their lives to God but this is precisely what God requires. It is unrighteous for us to run our own lives as if we are God. But that is what all people do. Their entire way of living is wrong. This is why God requires people to repent. The entire way of living must be turned completely around. Before salvation, people run their own lives. After salvation, Jesus is Lord (boss) and He runs their lives. This is not a matter to be taken lightly. This is why Jesus could use the type of language He used to drive the reality of this issue home. Unless a man is willing to die for Jesus, he cannot be His disciple. Jesus must be trusted (believed) even with our very lives. We must yield the ownership of them to Him and trust His direction and wisdom in all matters of life.

When a man lives this way, it proves that he really does believe the gospel of Jesus Christ. He really believes that just as Jesus was raised from the dead, so he too will be raised from the dead as Jesus promised. *"Jesus said to her, 'I am the resurrection and the life. He who believes in Me, though he may die, he shall live'" (John 11:25)*. True disciples of Jesus believe the following:

- That Jesus' death satisfied God's demand for punishment
- After they die, Jesus will raise them from the dead to live with Him forever (as He promised)

Because they really believe these things, disciples are willing to trust Jesus even with their physical lives to do with them and even dispose of them as He sees fit. They are willing even to endure suffering and persecution that results from being identified as one of Jesus' disciples.

The gospel invitation.

The gospel invitation is to anyone and everyone who wants to be saved. You cannot earn the gift of eternal life. To receive it, you simply must believe the gospel from your heart. But the only people who truly believe the gospel from their hearts are those who are willing to die for Jesus. If a person is unwilling to die for Jesus, it suggests that they really do not believe the gospel from their hearts.

Those who express a desire to become disciples of Jesus must first understand the implications or demands it has on their lives. They must first understand that when they become a disciple, they must resign the control of their lives to Jesus. They must not under estimate the implications. They must be told that when they identify themselves as disciples of Jesus, they will be ridiculed and undergo unjust treatment. They may suffer loss of property and even their physical lives simply because they are disciples of Jesus. They must be told that because of all these things, life will be difficult, not easy. And they must be told that only those who endure all these things to the end will ultimately be saved (resurrected to new life when Jesus comes back.) To all who understand the implications and still want to become disciples of Jesus Christ, His invitation is extended:

"Come unto me, all ye that labour and are heavy laden, and I will give you rest. Take my yoke upon you, and learn of me; for I am meek and lowly in heart: and ye shall find rest unto your souls. For my yoke is easy, and my burden is light" (Matthew 11:28-30 KJV).

All who believe the gospel from the heart should identify themselves as disciples of Jesus by being baptized. (If they are not willing to be baptized, they prove that they really do not believe the gospel because all who believe it gladly resign the ownership of their lives to Jesus.) Since He commanded us to be baptized true disciples will gladly be baptized in obedience to Him.

For more information about how to become a disciple of Jesus Christ, see my book, *The Gospel Guide to Safe Harbor for Your Soul- How to Become a Disciple of Jesus Christ.*

Other books by Tom Bear

Overcoming the Powers of Darkness -Using God's Spiritual Armor. It is the goal of our enemy to lull us into an apathetic, lukewarm spiritual existence. To obtain the abundant life, we cannot sit back passively and wait for God to spiritually zap us. We must engage in spiritual battle. In his epistle to the Ephesians, the Apostle Paul used imagery of a soldier's armor. Some have suggested that we engage in spiritual battle by mentioning the various pieces of this armor in a daily prayer. This is not true. Paul was teaching about spiritual principles that we must employ as a way of life. This book examines these spiritual principles and provides strong exhortation to increase our desire to live the abundant life that Jesus offers to us. (110 pages in paperback edition.)

The Gospel Guide to Safe Harbor for Your Soul- How to Become a Disciple of Jesus Christ: This book is written to help those who are concerned about what will happen to them after they die. Ideally, a Christian friend will use to this book to help those who want to learn to follow Jesus Christ. But even without such a friend, this book can still guide people through this process. This book unashamedly teaches that the gospel of Jesus Christ is THE WAY and the only way of salvation that God has provided. It does not attempt to argue, debate or prove it. It merely proclaims it as true and presents it as the remedy all people need. There are three standalone parts: Part One: Learn the gospel and come to agreement with it. -Part Two: The appropriate response to the gospel. -Part Three: Your ongoing response to the gospel. Readers should progress through this book one part at a time and at their own pace. At the end of each part, there are a few questions that can be answered from the material covered in that part. Answers to these questions are available in the back of the book. By God's grace, readers will learn the gospel of Jesus Christ and then become disciples of Jesus Christ and eventually spend eternity with Him. This book can help parents guide their children to the way of salvation. Also, Christians can help their unbelieving friends learn how to become a disciple of Jesus by giving them a copy of this book. (100 pages in paperback format.)

How to Evangelize- Bringing Back the Gospel: In the 21st century, many evangelism techniques are being used that have no biblical foundation. *Bringing Back the Gospel*, examines the Bible to determine what Christians should and should not do in order to fulfill the Great Commission. Christians all over the world consider this book an excellent instructional resource that is firmly grounded in the Bible. (154 pages in paperback format.)

Bring My Sheep Back: Church Discipline, the Loving Way presents a candid framework for the process of restoring Christians that stray. Most of the books that deal with this subject approach it from the standpoint of solving conflicts between Christians. *Bring My Sheep Back* is founded on Jesus' teaching to put the interests of the straying Christian ahead of our own desire for immediate relief of pain caused by the one caught in sin. Personal observations along with much attention to biblical instruction produce a very useful and thorough resource for church leaders and lay people who desire to restore Christians trapped by sin. This book warns against dependence on man-made approaches to solving relational problems. Whether it involves private sin or public scandal, or even cases that involve the governing authorities, biblical principles are taught as foundational to the process of restoration. (130 pages in paperback format.)

Christian Marriage: This book provides biblical principles that if applied, will result in harmony in the marriage and glory to God. Some will undoubtedly say that many problems in marriage are far too complex for such a short book to address. It is the premise of this book, however, that the source of all problems in Christian marriages are the result of failure to live as God has taught us to live in His Word. If a Christian couple lives in accordance with God's principles described in *Christian Marriage*, true harmony is guaranteed. (50 pages in paperback edition)

The Way to Heaven- The Difference Between Islam and Christianity:
Like many people, you may be under the impression that the Bible and the Koran generally teach that to get to heaven, a person must achieve a certain level of "goodness" by doing more good things than bad things. In reality, each teaches an opposing view about the way to heaven. This book is written to explain the difference between these two messages while attempting to explain how most Muslims think about this matter. Tom Bear has been an evangelical Christian since 1975. During the past several years, he has spoken with thousands of Muslims face to face, one on one, at great length about their understanding of God and the gospel of Jesus Christ. This book is based upon this experience and his understanding of the gospel of Jesus Christ. (60 Pages in paperback format.)

Evangelism Fuel- Motivation to Evangelize: It is spontaneous praise and testimony of the wonder of Jesus that forms the basis of our witness of Jesus Christ in this world. This type of witness requires the supernatural power of the Holy Spirit to be unleashed in us. It is not something that we can produce in our own strength. The Holy Spirit must be freely moving in us to produce a life that experiences the power and person of Jesus Christ. As we come in contact with His glory in this way, we will have much reason and motivation to testify to the wonder of Jesus. This book is written in a devotional style with short, heart-felt meditations that can be read in just a few minutes each day. These meditations are intended to help believers understand the supernatural work God calls them to do and motivate them to seek and experience God's glory in it. (72 pages in paperback format.)

The Local Church: Most pastors wish that the members of their churches would grow and flourish more. The church members often sense that God has purposes for them but they don't know what He wants them to do. They often end up playing the role of an unfulfilled spectator. *The Local Church* examines the early New Testament Church and its teachings for answers to this universal problem. It demonstrates how certain unbiblical attitudes and traditions exist which cultivate this unhealthy spectator mindset. *The Local Church* challenges leaders and "laypeople" to identify and discard these unbiblical attitudes and practices that stifle spiritual health. This book asserts that if the pattern of the early New Testament Church is followed today, Christians will mature at a greater pace and experience fulfillment as active participants in the advancement of Christ's Kingdom. (160 pages in paperback format.)

Birth Control: A Spiritual Shackle- Did you know that before the twentieth century, the Protestant Church boldly spoke out against the practice of birth control? They were opposed to any act of man that interfered with the natural order of procreation. Men such as John Calvin, Martin Luther, John Wesley, Arthur Pink and Augustine were vehemently opposed to birth control. Today, Birth control is not just tolerated, it is embraced by the Protestant Church. Why has the Protestant Church changed its position? Is it possible that Christians living before the twentieth century were all mistaken? Why did they take a stand against birth control? Is it possible that the church of the nineteenth century was better equipped to discern right from wrong? Using six biblical arguments, this book demonstrates that birth control is a worldly practice that opposes God's will for His people, violates the marriage covenant and is an attack on the very character of God. (64 pages in paperback format.)

Toward the Celestial City- The Lives of Tom and Linda Bear: We look like ordinary people who live in an ordinary home in an ordinary neighborhood. If you read this book, you will conclude that our lives have NOT been ordinary. On the one hand, you will read how two people made such an extraordinary mess of their lives resulting in hopeless drug addiction and an utterly ruined marriage. On the other hand, you will see how God transformed all the garbage that we created into a glorious display of His love and power. *"Behold, I make all things new."* As you read our story, you will find some things astounding, some miraculous, some hilarious, some things uplifting and some things sad. This book bears witness to the fact that God continually makes Himself known to His children though the things He does and the way He does them. *"The works of the LORD are great, studied by all who have pleasure in them" (Psalm 111:2).* If it were not for His loving, providential involvement in every aspect of our lives, we would **only know about Him** and we would not actually **know Him personally**. It is our hope that this book will allow the reader to see how God has made Himself known to us personally through the events and circumstances of our lives. We believe you will be encouraged as you read about the many awesome answers to prayer which clearly demonstrate that God is powerful and actively working in the lives of His children. (160 pages in paperback format.)

Made in the USA
Lexington, KY
16 July 2017